LITTLE BIT OF YOU.
LITTLE BIT OF ME.

MARY MAGDALINA= ISHIKA MANDELIA

ISBN 979-888555080-2

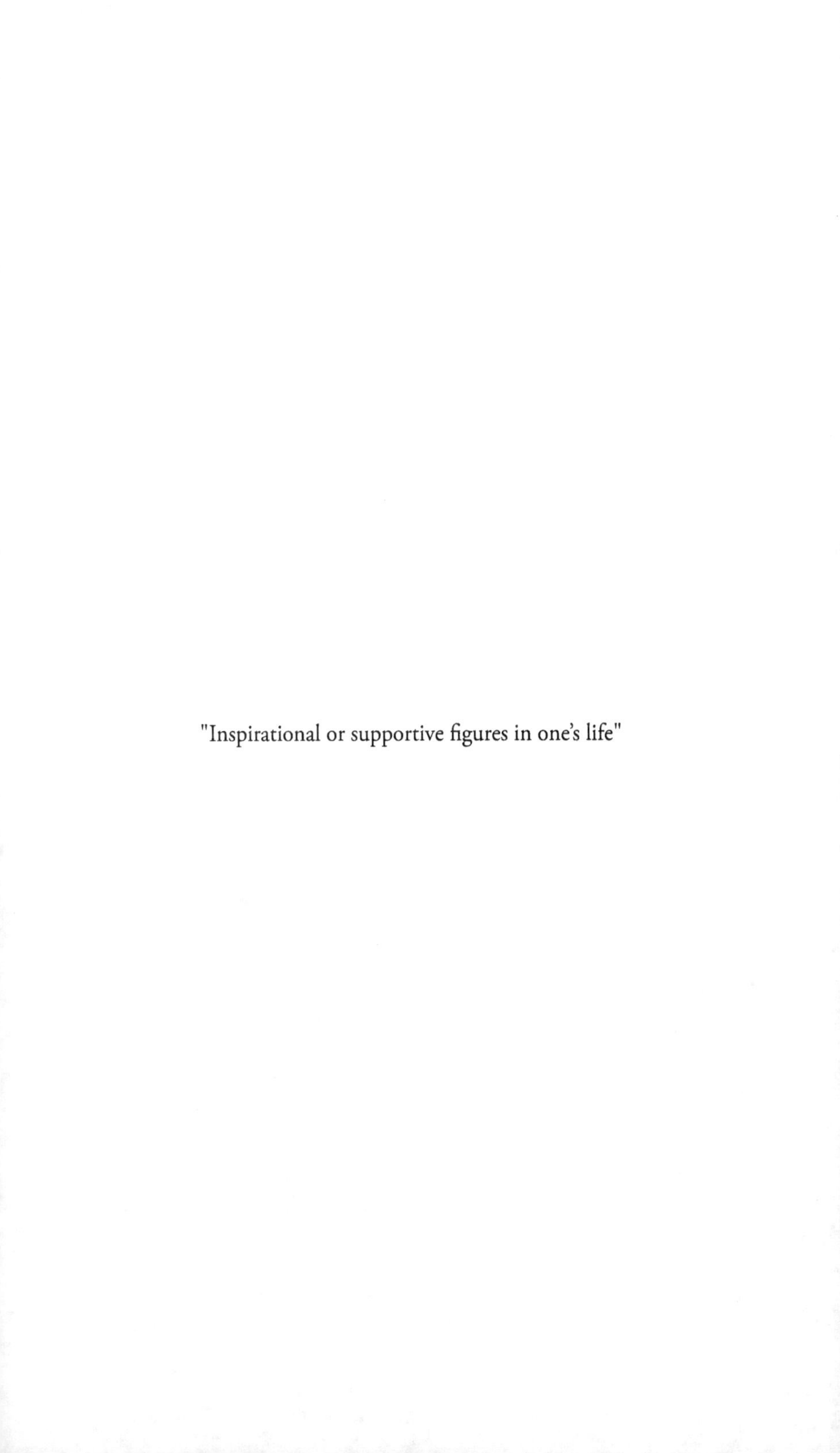

"Inspirational or supportive figures in one's life"

Contents

Contents

Contents

Preface

PREFACE

Life is a constant state of learning, relearning, feeling and understanding. A thousand feelings and a million thoughts, altogether form who we are. Each of us walk our own unique paths, yet there are junctions in our journey, where we seem to know each other as if we have spent a lifetime together. 'A little bit of you, a little bit of me' will find way to your heart in several ways and perhaps help you through your journey.

About The Author.

<u>Mary Magdalina.</u>

you see this smile on my face that's because she
loves to do what she want...
Call her Mary Magdalina from India born on
oct 29, currently staying in Hyderabad pursuing
Bsc Nursing course In Kims college of Nursing.
Started writing poems when she was broken down
but today she stands to inspire people through her
words.
Not only poems she also started writing non-fiction
books
1.THE CALL OF TRUTH
2.WHOM WILL YOU CHOOSE? GOD or DOOM
3. WALK INTO THE LIGHT
4.WHY?
5.THE WHOLE ME.
from a very small stage she begin her journey and
is blessed to be a writer.

About The Author

ISHIKA MANDELIA

She is Ishika Mandelia.
Born on 05-03-2002 in the sunny state of Telangana, India. She is a daughter, sister and a friend to many.
She is pursuing chartered accountancy and enjoys reading and writing poetry, and upcycling.
Awards: All rounder award by the rotary club of Hyderabad, best change agent award in the climate change program by HSBC.

Acknowledgements

First I would like to thank My friend for working with me for the dream of writing a book. She has helped me with all the ideas and glad to meet such an amazing writer.This book wouldn't have been possible without her. As the main concept of the book and the best title was given from her.

We never thought that we would work but god has made two friends to publish this wonderful book.

I'd also like to thank the Publishers who have helped us to publish this wonderful book.

We are also are very greatful for the wonderful parents who has supported us to follow our dream.

I'm also immensely grateful to you who has taken this book and are supporting us to move further. We are really happy to publish this book and we hope that this book has made you fill the little of us in you too..

cause it's LITTLE BIT OF YOU AND LITTLE BIT OF ME.

THANKYOU.

Little Bit of you-Little Bit of Me

Poetry is not all about the rhyme

It's about the words that carry

A little bit of skin, a little bit of bone

A little bit of you, a little bit of me.

Hug

' What lives inside a hug? '

An abandoned house stands
Frozen in time, so still
A dusky ray of light
Flies home a kite.

A wild flower blooms, in black
and blue
Exhaling love, in red and pink.
A timely thorn, scars and
bruises
Grounded roots, heal and
snooze.

A company incorporates
From your veins and my cells
An amalgamation , it is
Of your fantasies and my
dreams.

What lives inside a hug
Knows not you nor me
How tight is a tight tug
Wonder thy fingers
Bonding on a sewing spree.

A Warrior Spirit

Far Beyond my scars,
underneath all of the
bruises,
lives a warrior spirit.

A spirit so strong,
that it never loses hope,
it continues to fight
the never ending battle
of this life.

With You

You cannot die, you just cannot
Because, you promised me a lifetime
And I'm not ready to live it by myself
Because, with you next to me
It's warmer than my cup of tea
Because, 'we' haven't had enough time
And I'm not sure about life after death
Because, i don't wanna look for you
In each of the 200 different things
A poem means, to the 200 different people
Because, no one can make me smile
Like you, as wide as a mile
Because, I don't wanna trip and fall
Cause your arms are where I belong, after all.

King_Queen

alone,under the moon,
she awaits her King, The kiss
that makes her swoon.
she prays to the stars to watch
over
their dreams, so
she can be his queen.

Me.

I DON'T EXACTLY KNOW ITS GENRE
BUT ITS A KIND OF LATENT EMOTION ,
SHOWS UP ON ANY FINE DAY
AND MANAGES TO TURN IT INTO DRY HAY.
JUST AS MY ELATION COMES TO CONTOUR ,
I AM REMINDED OF ITS UNHEALTHY ESSENCE ,
HITCHED BACK INTO A PLETHORA OF DARK MESS.
AS THE SALT WATERS BEGAN TO MARK THEIR TERRITORY,
A BREATH SO CALM IS PROHIBITED FROM TRESPASSING .
IN THE NAME OF A BAD DAY,
ONCE AGAIN MY COMPASSION IS STOLEN ,
PERSISTENT VILIFICATION IS ALL THAT REMAINS.
AMIDS THE FADING REALITY
IT FEELS LIKE
I'M CRUCIFIED TO THE PLAIN WHITE THOUGHTS
MORTIFIED BY THE CONSUMING ,PITCH BLACK DARKNESS
AND HIGH ON BLOOD RED EMOTIONS
WHICH I JUST COULD NOT CLEARLY CONTEMPLATE
SO NAMED THEM NAMELESS.

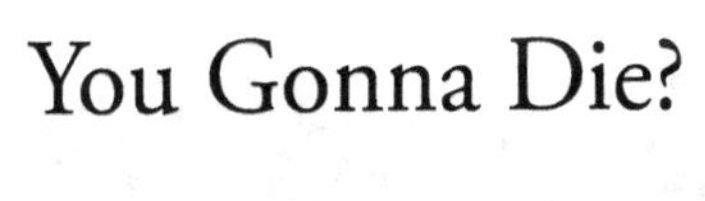# You Gonna Die?

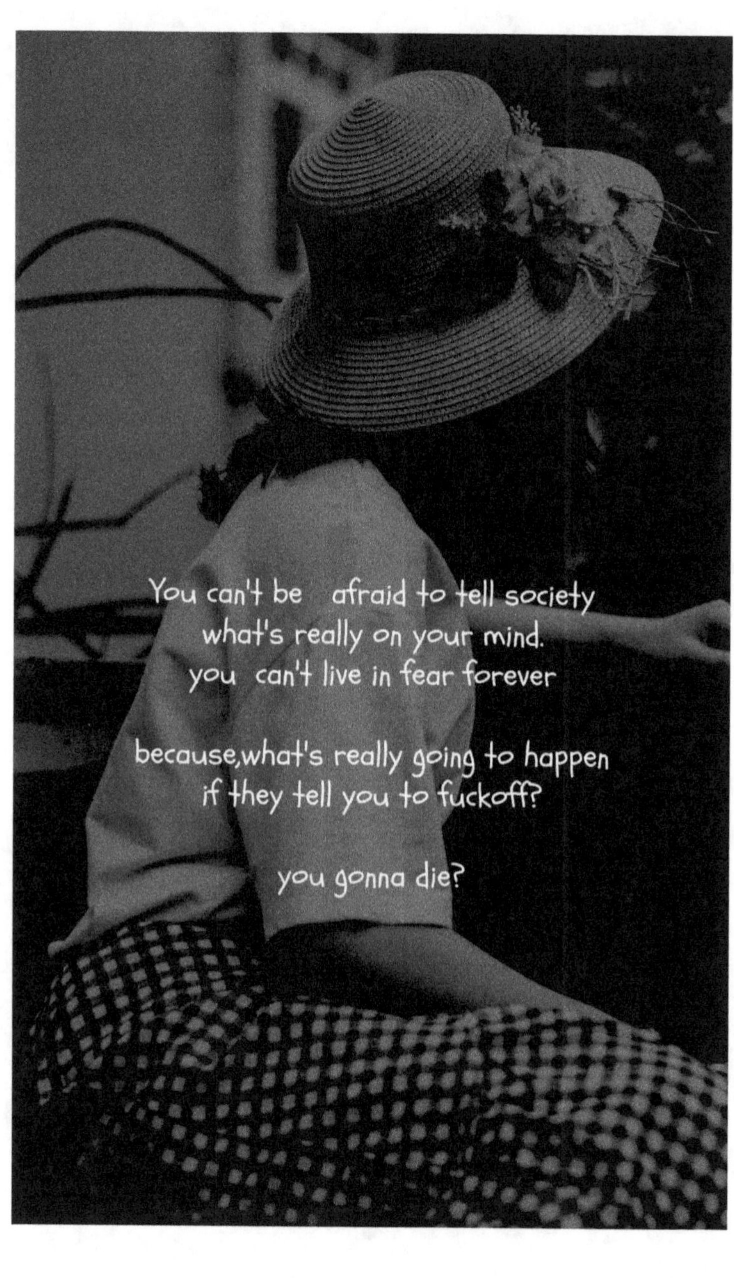
You can't be   afraid to tell society
what's really on your mind.
you can't live in fear forever

because,what's really going to happen
if they tell you to fuckoff?

you gonna die?

Gilded Moments

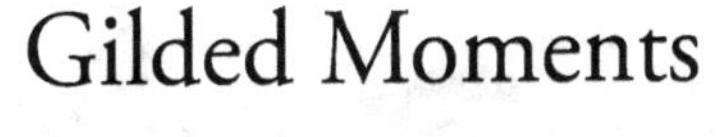

'GILDED MOMENTS.'

ALL I REMEMBER IS
WHEN I WAS WITH YOU
I COULD FORGET EVERYTHING IN LESS THAN A SECOND
AND LIKE AN IMBECILE
I JUST WOULDN'T STOP SMILING EVEN AFTER MY CHEEKS ACHE .
WHEN I WAS STANDING WITH YOU
I WAS TOO HAPPY TO BE SAD
DID NOT HAVE A CARE IN THE WORLD
I AM NOT SURE IF IT WAS YOUR AURA
OR THE LOVE TAINTED AMBIENCE.
WHEN I WAS JUST NEXT TO YOU
I WAS SO CONTENTED IN THE MOMENT
I'D STRUGGLE TO FRAME A SENTENCE
SO OVERWHELMED - FELT LIKE I COULD LACERATE THROUGH
EVERYTHING AND JUST BE ECSTATIC FOREVER.
IT WAS DIABOLICAL.
MAYBE I WAS SO NONCHALANT
THAT I HAD MISTAKEN YOU FOR MY TALISMAN.
ALTHOUGH THEY'RE TARNISHED
IF I COULD I WISH TO RELIVE
WHAT I CALL 'THE GILDED MOMENTS.'

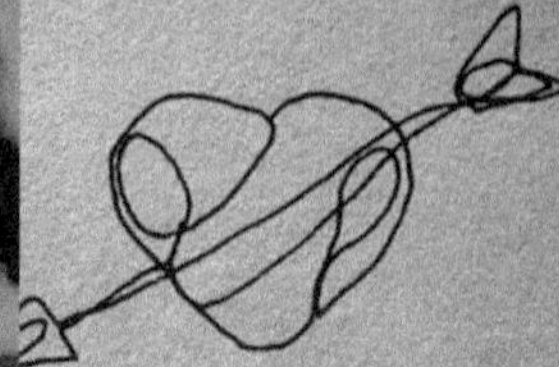

It's You I Choose.

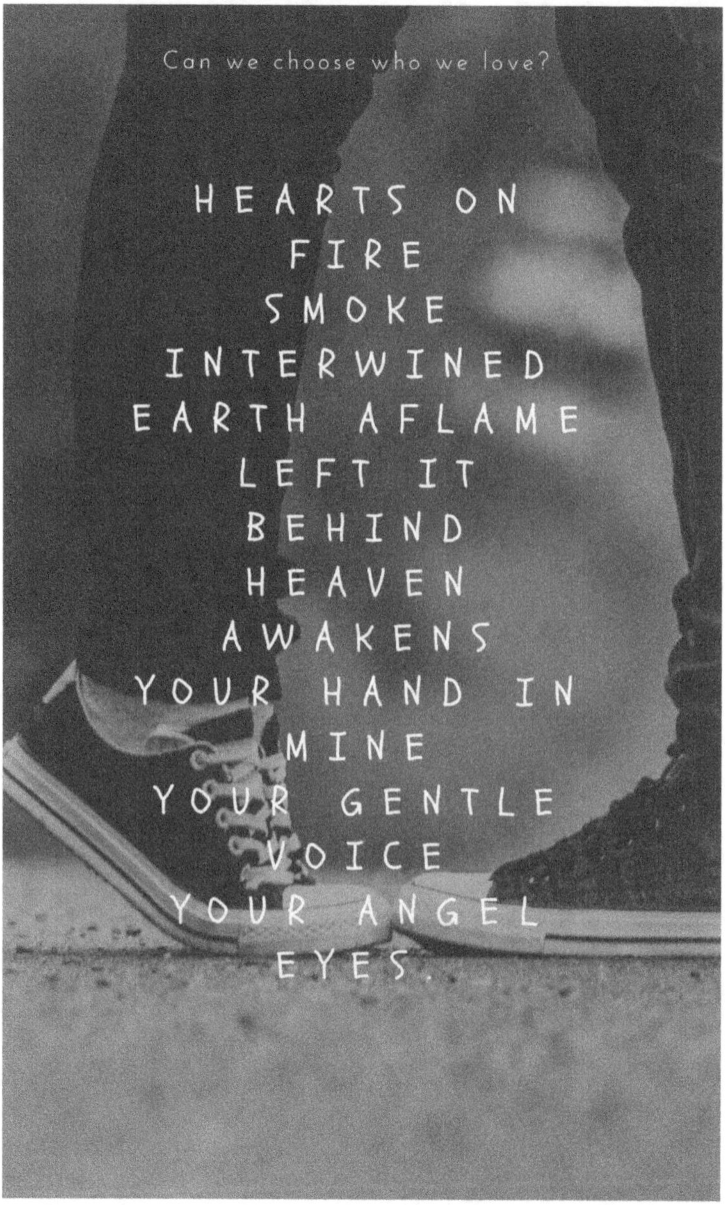
Can we choose who we love?
HEARTS ON
FIRE
SMOKE
INTERWINED
EARTH AFLAME
LEFT IT
BEHIND
HEAVEN
AWAKENS
YOUR HAND IN
MINE
YOUR GENTLE
VOICE
YOUR ANGEL
EYES.

Darkness.

I SHUT MY EYES AND LIE DOWN
BUT MY BONES ACHE FOR REST
I'VE BEEN TO VARIOUS PLACES
WITH MY BRAIN
RUNNING LIKE A NON STOP TRAIN
MY EYELIDS ARE A CANVAS
AND LASHES ITS EASEL
MY EYES HAVE PAINTED SO MUCH
AND HAVE BEEN PAINTING
EVERY NIGHT
NOW ITS ALL A MESSY STORY
I HIDE UNDER THE EYELIDS
AND PUSH IT ALL BACK
TO THE ARCHIVE WITH A EYE ROLE
BEFORE ITS MORNING.

Voices.

There is voices in my head who can relate
How am I feeling?
They talk to me as they knew me
But i can't talk to them forever
otherwise, people would call me crazy.
I am surrounding whom i called family but
they can't accept as i wanna be.
I called to my voices and claimed as they
are for me,always be with them that i
ever wanna be.

Memories

all our memories reside at the sea side
braided along the waves and powered by the currents
migrating from place to place,
everywhere leaving a hint of trace
living all the things that could have been
and the fantasized reality
our future could have seen.

Grow to myself

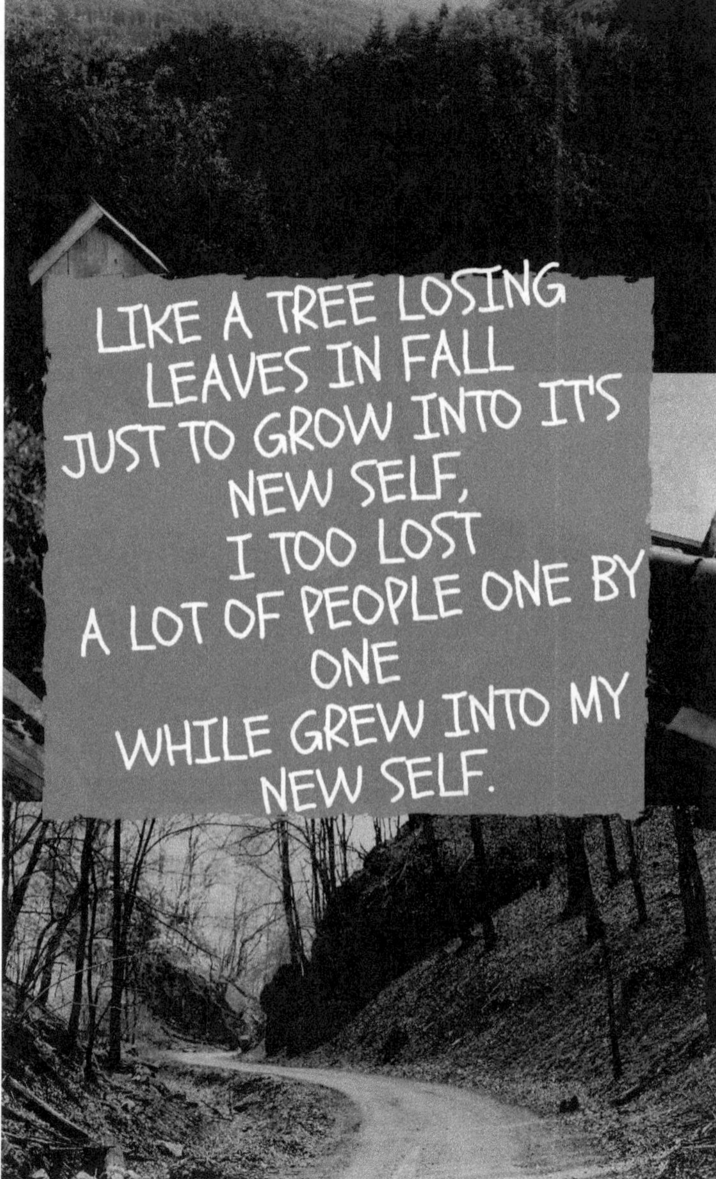
LIKE A TREE LOSING
LEAVES IN FALL
JUST TO GROW INTO IT'S
NEW SELF,
I TOO LOST
A LOT OF PEOPLE ONE BY
ONE
WHILE GREW INTO MY
NEW SELF.

Peace

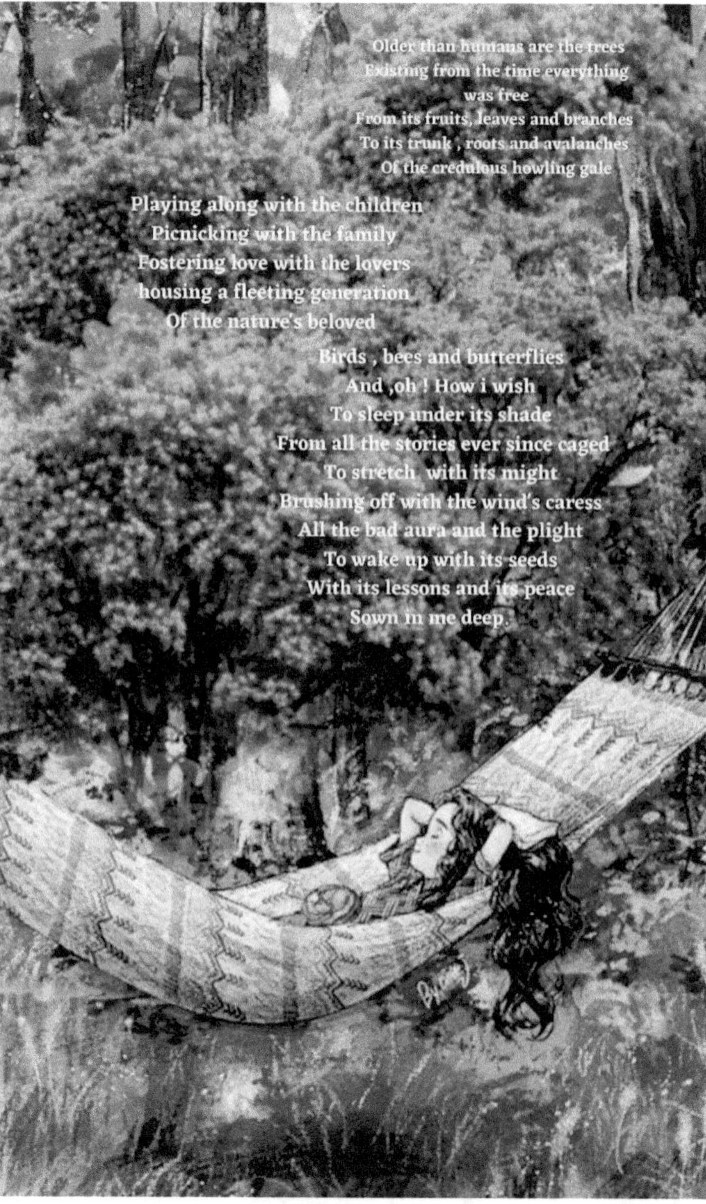

Older than humans are the trees
Existing from the time everything
was free
From its fruits, leaves and branches
To its trunk , roots and avalanches
Of the credulous howling gale

Playing along with the children
Picnicking with the family
Fostering love with the lovers
housing a fleeting generation
Of the nature's beloved

Birds , bees and butterflies
And ,oh ! How i wish
To sleep under its shade
From all the stories ever since caged
To stretch with its might
Brushing off with the wind's caress
All the bad aura and the plight
To wake up with its seeds
With its lessons and its peace
Sown in me deep.

Sainy.

you call me a fallen woman
as if i was once an angel in the
sky

you name me a sainy
as if you love me more when i
suffer

you call me brave
as if my sacrifices were
willingly made

Ask.

Ask!
What love means to a person who chose to
stay. Always.
Ask!
What death means to a person who'd swap
lives with a dying stranger.

Ask!
What a bottleneck is. To an introvert
who no longer can keep it all in.
Ask !
If words could scream internally. To the
walls of a ghost town.

Ask!
About everything that's hidden behind the rosy
smile of the sky!
Ask!
About all that the wind has given up to flow
persistently, to come this far.

Ask!
A star , how dark could a life be.
Ask!
A blanket, how cold could the world outside be.
Ask!
The roots, if everything was a trap all this time.

Ask!
A soul, how it feels like to slowly kill itself from
within.
Ask!
Yourself, how it feels like to loose the favorite
version of you.

Ask!
A human, how it feels like to not feel human
anymore.

If I Stop?

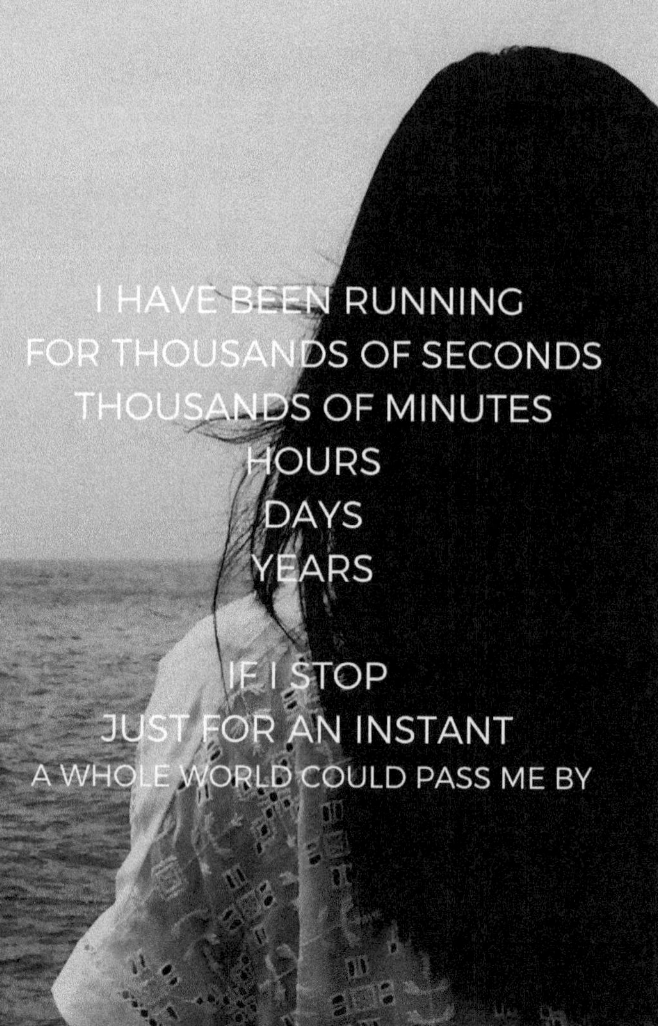
I HAVE BEEN RUNNING
FOR THOUSANDS OF SECONDS
THOUSANDS OF MINUTES
HOURS
DAYS
YEARS

IF I STOP
JUST FOR AN INSTANT
A WHOLE WORLD COULD PASS ME BY

Cemetery Of Smiles

"Cemetery of smiles "

Before the sky retires
Through one more night
Will you please , dear Stars
Take me back
To the cemetery of smiles
Maybe I can stitch a tatter
From the smiles I barter
Show the moon
The parts death couldn't wipe
And the fine tune
Of the memories that ripe
Plant my favorite colours
In the butterfly cocoons
and promise of your return
Till its next june
Contour the winds
Through the galaxy
And swing with violins
Into a blur of reality.

Breath In Vaccum

LOVING
YOU FELT
LIKE
DYING ON
THE MOON
I WAS
IN THE
PRESENCE
OF
SOMETHING
BEAUTIFUL
YET
GASPING
FOR
BREATH
IN A
SPACE
VACCUM.

The Ray Of Hope

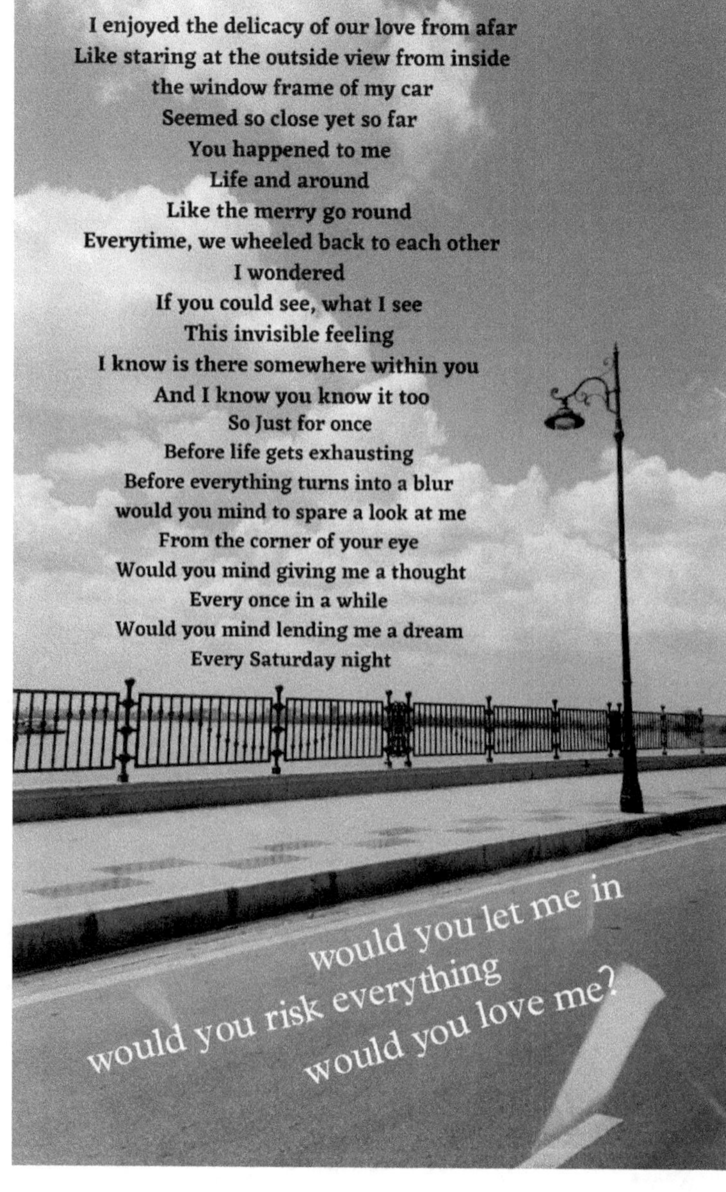

I enjoyed the delicacy of our love from afar
Like staring at the outside view from inside
the window frame of my car
Seemed so close yet so far
You happened to me
Life and around
Like the merry go round
Everytime, we wheeled back to each other
I wondered
If you could see, what I see
This invisible feeling
I know is there somewhere within you
And I know you know it too
So Just for once
Before life gets exhausting
Before everything turns into a blur
would you mind to spare a look at me
From the corner of your eye
Would you mind giving me a thought
Every once in a while
Would you mind lending me a dream
Every Saturday night
would you let me in
would you risk everything
would you love me?

Deeper Into Dreams

Deeper Dreams into

I live in shades of
blue,
a little broken,
a little lacking,
waiting for the light
to right the wrongs.

It's Me In Agony

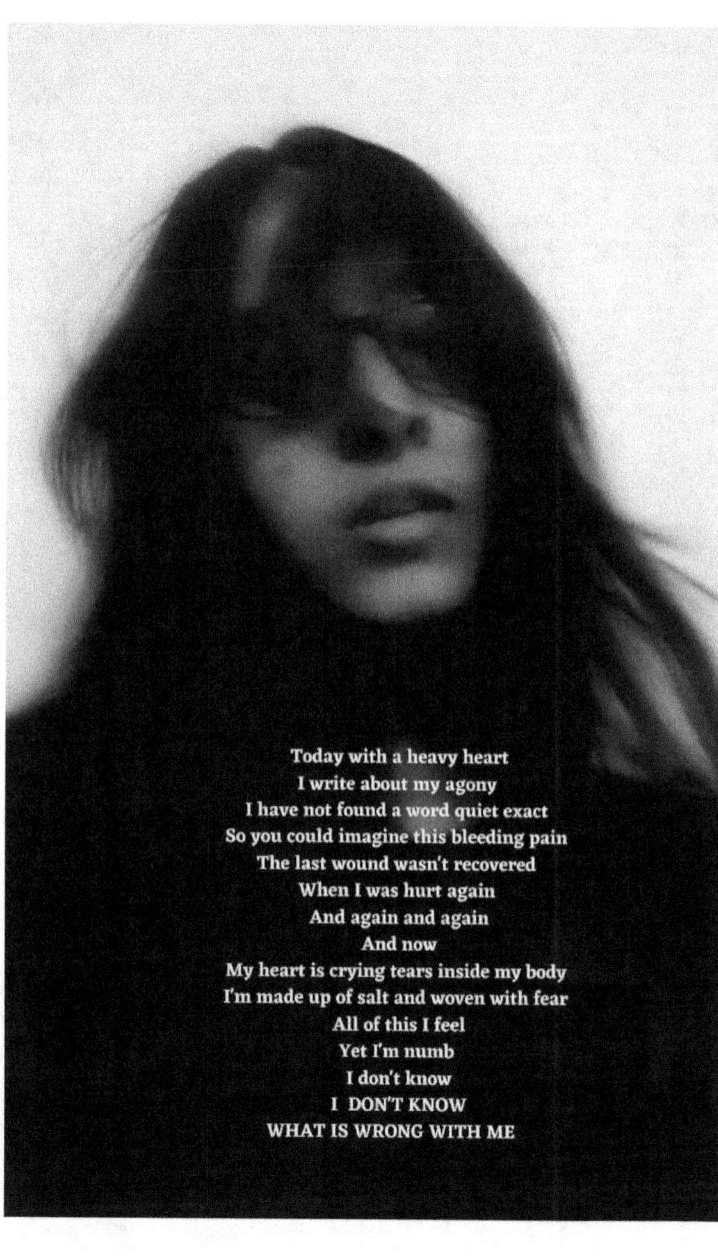

Today with a heavy heart
I write about my agony
I have not found a word quiet exact
So you could imagine this bleeding pain
The last wound wasn't recovered
When I was hurt again
And again and again
And now
My heart is crying tears inside my body
I'm made up of salt and woven with fear
All of this I feel
Yet I'm numb
I don't know
I DON'T KNOW
WHAT IS WRONG WITH ME

My Journey

I should be working on
myself
no giving up to find
peace
healing is a long
journey
but
trust me
once you're there
it's the best feeling ever

World's Million Starts

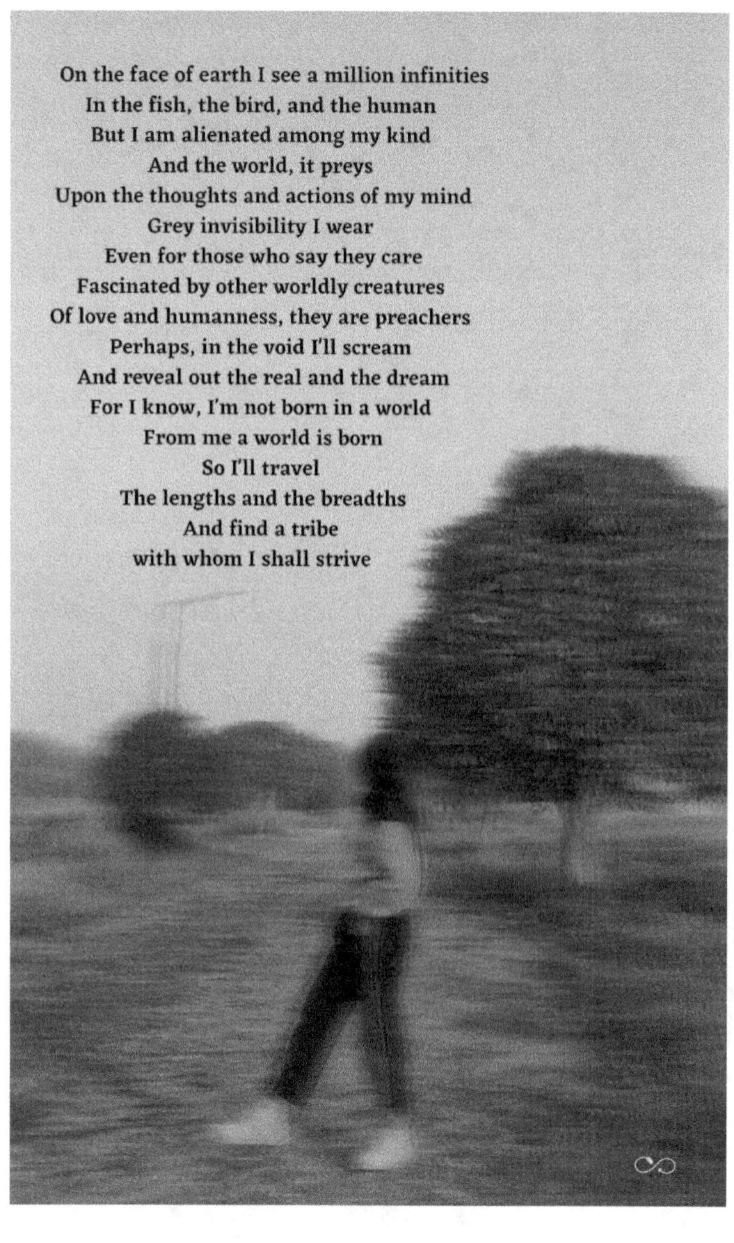

On the face of earth I see a million infinities
In the fish, the bird, and the human
But I am alienated among my kind
And the world, it preys
Upon the thoughts and actions of my mind
Grey invisibility I wear
Even for those who say they care
Fascinated by other worldly creatures
Of love and humanness, they are preachers
Perhaps, in the void I'll scream
And reveal out the real and the dream
For I know, I'm not born in a world
From me a world is born
So I'll travel
The lengths and the breadths
And find a tribe
with whom I shall strive

Grave.

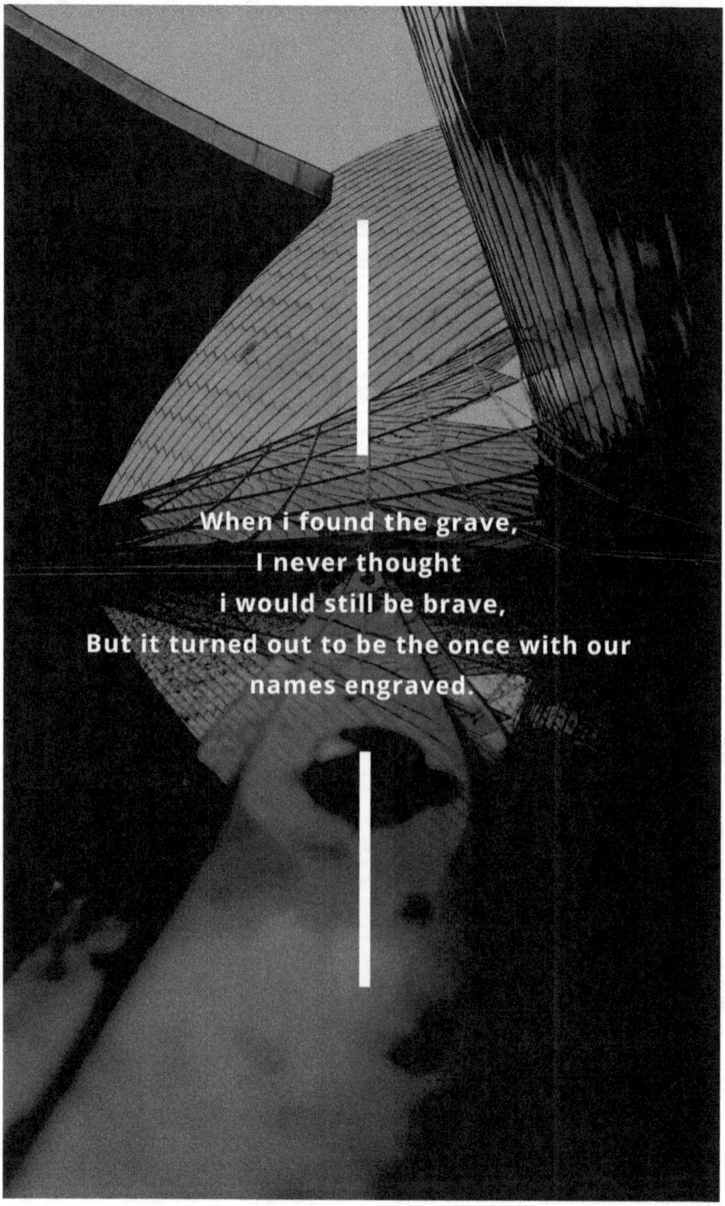

When i found the grave,
I never thought
i would still be brave,
But it turned out to be the once with our
names engraved.

Human

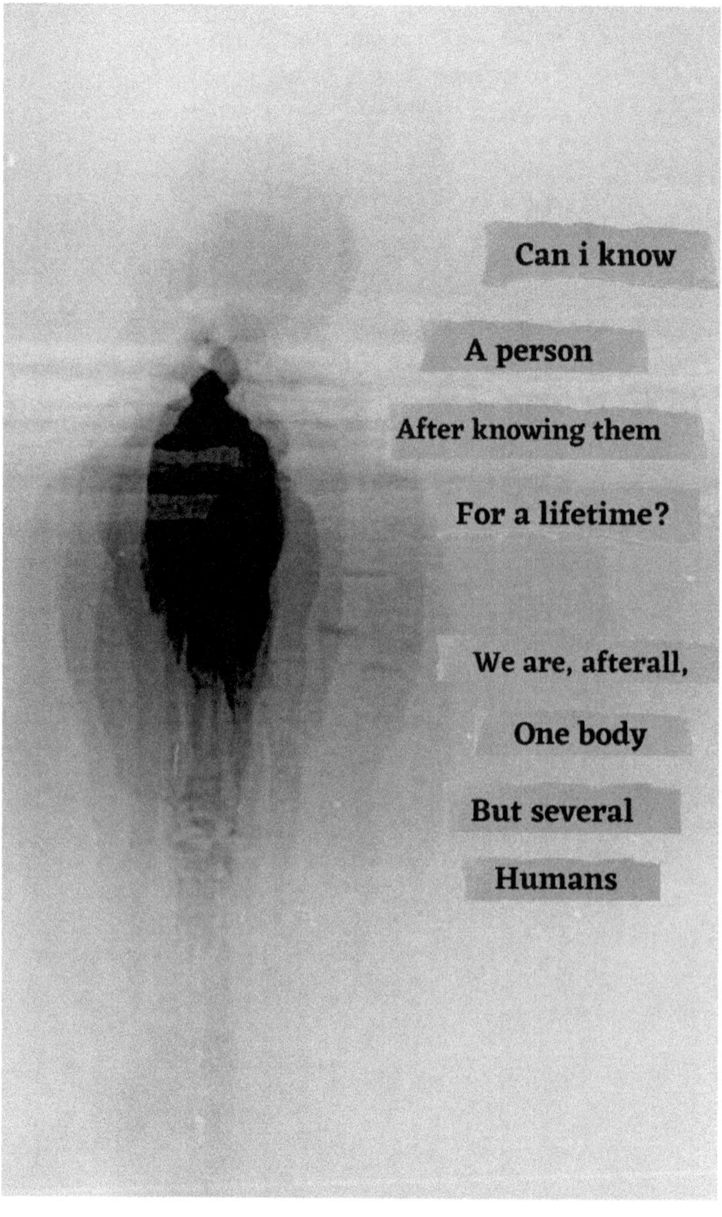

Can i know

A person

After knowing them

For a lifetime?

We are, afterall,

One body

But several

Humans

The Armor.

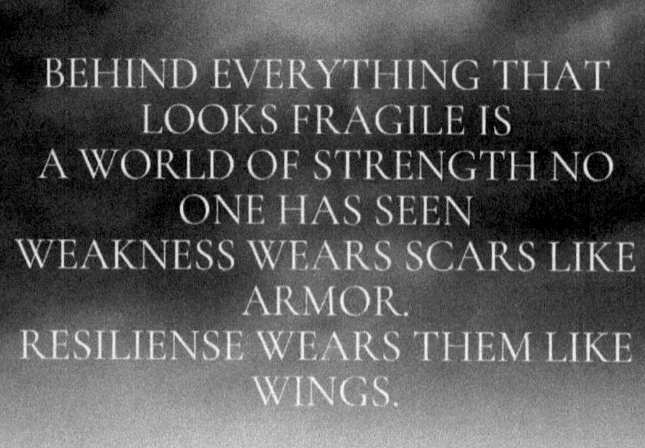

BEHIND EVERYTHING THAT
LOOKS FRAGILE IS
A WORLD OF STRENGTH NO
ONE HAS SEEN
WEAKNESS WEARS SCARS LIKE
ARMOR.
RESILIENSE WEARS THEM LIKE
WINGS.

Flower

The dried flower pressed with wax
on your last letter
Was once blooming and fresh
with your memories and summer
Altogether.

ME

Show me where it hurts.
And let me show you
how I intend to make it stop.
I know sometime
There is a hell inside of you
I want it all.
all of it
all of you.

let me love the demons out of you.

Body

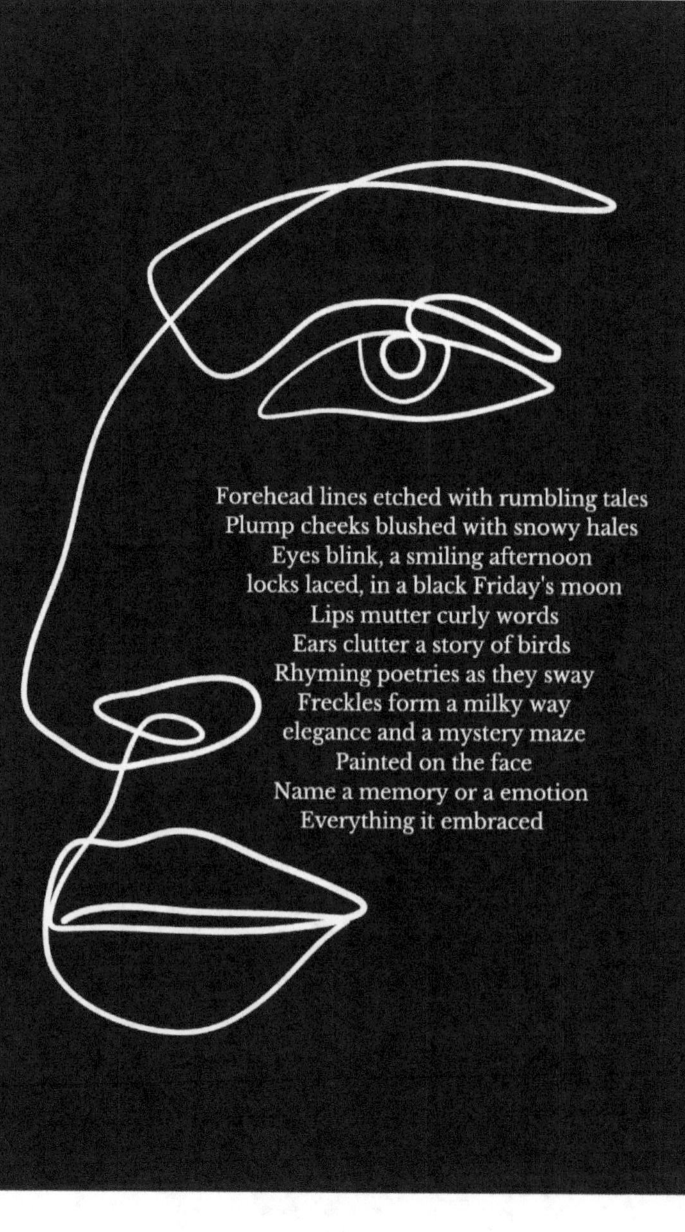

Forehead lines etched with rumbling tales
Plump cheeks blushed with snowy hales
Eyes blink, a smiling afternoon
locks laced, in a black Friday's moon
Lips mutter curly words
Ears clutter a story of birds
Rhyming poetries as they sway
Freckles form a milky way
elegance and a mystery maze
Painted on the face
Name a memory or a emotion
Everything it embraced

Older Version

"your older version
does not deserve to live a life of
regret
only because you were fearful,
To place your dream into reality"

Lights

The world is a plethora of abyss

Hence.in someways I understand

I'll remain a beginner

The world is a plethora of abyss

Love To Hate

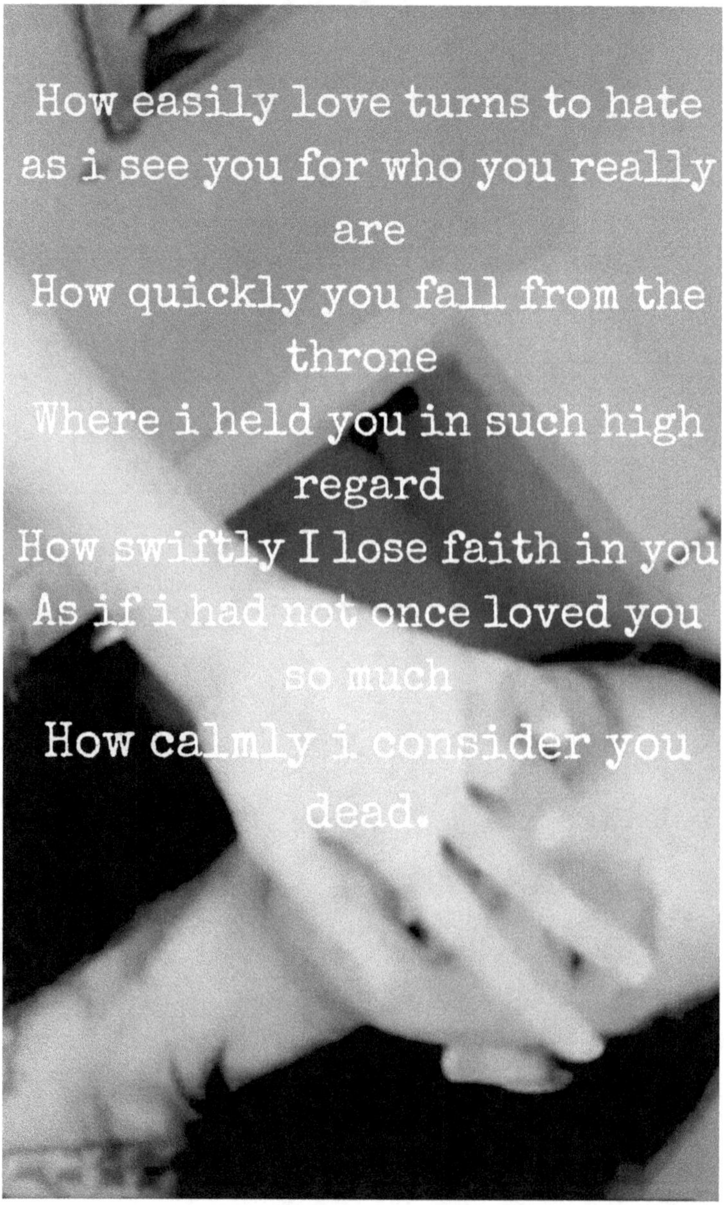

How easily love turns to hate
as i see you for who you really
are
How quickly you fall from the
throne
Where i held you in such high
regard
How swiftly I lose faith in you
As if i had not once loved you
so much
How calmly i consider you
dead.

World A Drama

There's drama everywhere
Inside you, me and the nature
For, without it there wouldn't be

Any happy, sad or excited
Or raging oceans and fiery clouds
There wouldn't be any art

The earth would be
People, tree and the ground
From the start

And, a war, I would wage
But you say,
All drama must remain
on the stage

Winter

warm
winter
"but maybe
just maybe...
we could have built
a home
in a hell
together"

Snow

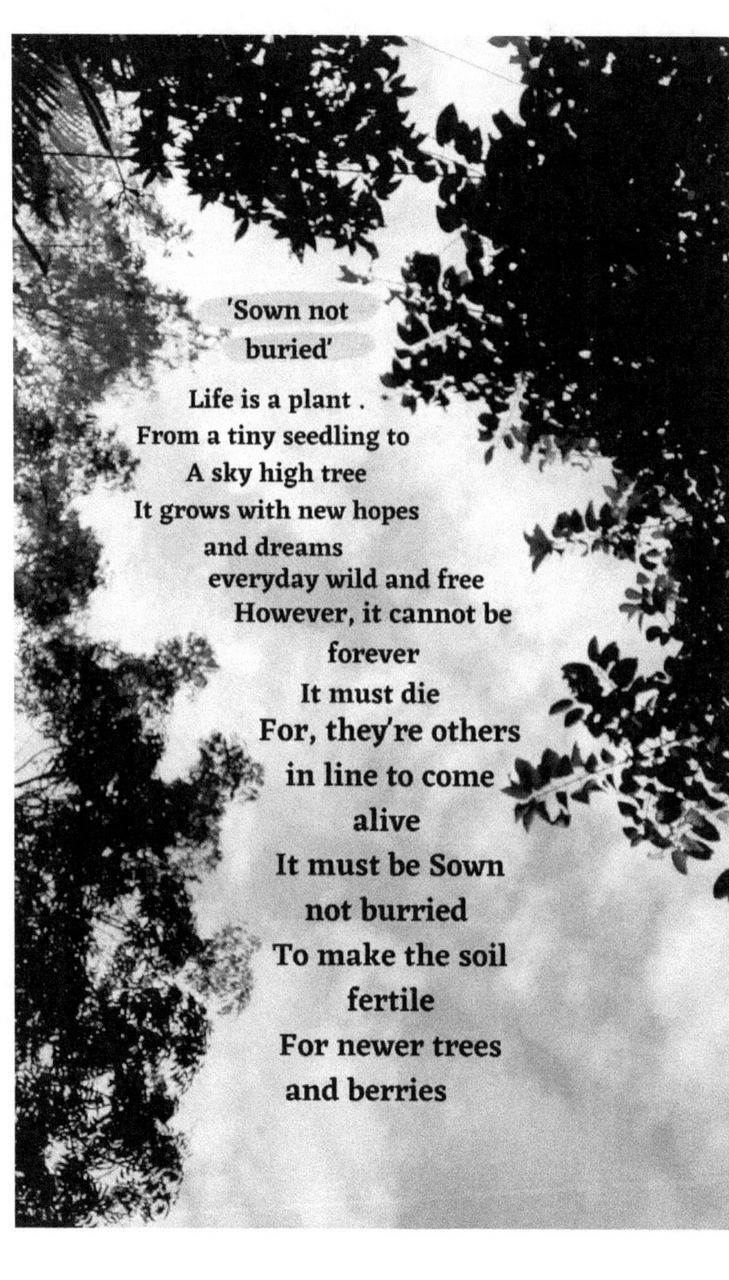

'Sown not
buried'

Life is a plant .
From a tiny seedling to
A sky high tree
It grows with new hopes
and dreams
everyday wild and free
However, it cannot be
forever
It must die
For, they're others
in line to come
alive
It must be Sown
not burried
To make the soil
fertile
For newer trees
and berries

WEB LIFE

Wild and carefree
is how I always imagined you
to be
beautifully untamed
my sun chaser
my adventure seeker
how lucky i am
to have held your heart
inside me

Rainbow

Agony makes you unfamiliar
with the rainbow
and familier with the rain
Even the sky needs rest and sleep
Some warmth and peace
So together stand , tall and high
Just one more day
And you'll ignore the grey , you'll
ignore the rain
You'll climb the rainbow and embrace
the pain.

A Smile of Rays

A cloud of sadness,
That covers my happiness.
It does not let me see the sun's
rays,
It does not let me breathe
An unexpected brightness
dazzles,
A big smile and warm hands,
They give me back that lost
happiness,
They were the same as I felt,
The first time I started crying.

Spices

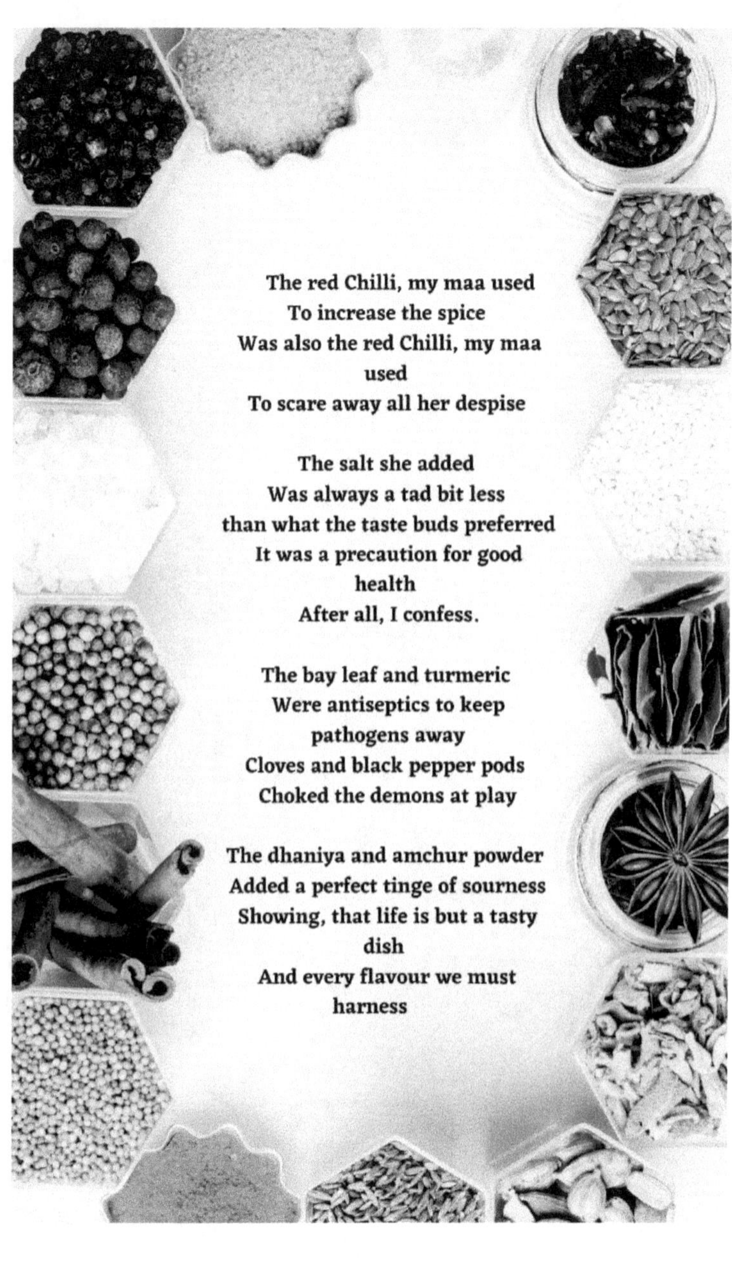

The red Chilli, my maa used
To increase the spice
Was also the red Chilli, my maa
used
To scare away all her despise

The salt she added
Was always a tad bit less
than what the taste buds preferred
It was a precaution for good
health
After all, I confess.

The bay leaf and turmeric
Were antiseptics to keep
pathogens away
Cloves and black pepper pods
Choked the demons at play

The dhaniya and amchur powder
Added a perfect tinge of sourness
Showing, that life is but a tasty
dish
And every flavour we must
harness

The Chess

We write scream
March and fight
Equality is our right

Its true, it is
Everyone's, her and his

We watch admire
Judge and hate
Does love carry so much
weight?

It does, for sure
people call it the cure

We say we believe
Yet so mean and wrong
Is beauty so hard to look at ?

Agreed that world is a mess
But not a game of chess

You're only missing a move
To look you don't approve

If only you would
You could see
The soldier could be
the next checkmate too.

The Road Way To Hope

'Hope' is the thing with feathers
—
That perches in the soul—
And sings the tune without the
words—
And never stops—at all—

Poetries

If the winds can laugh and oceans, dance
Then I shall name agony - an art
If the sun can love and moon, smile
Then I shall grow a sunflower heart

If the winter is doom and
summer, hope
Then I shall paint grey
rainbows and call them blue
If the time could stop and
forever, exist
Then I'll shall live in
poetries, a few.

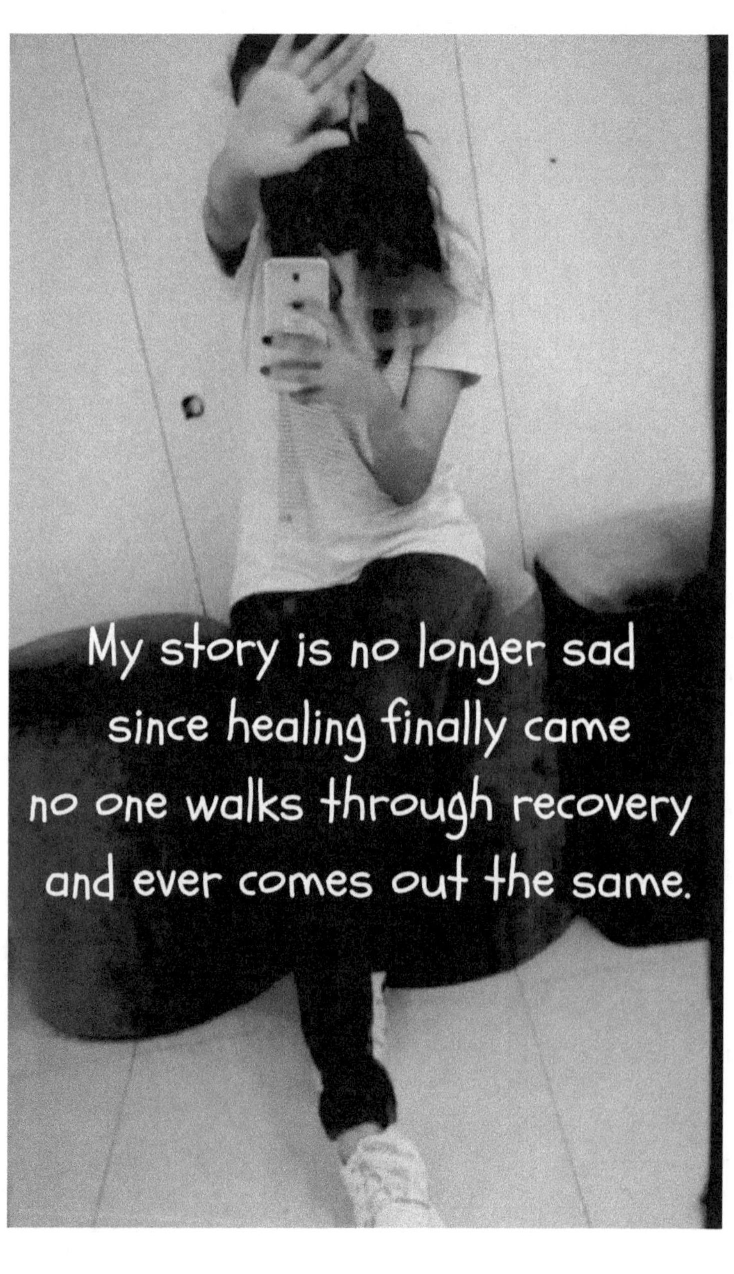
My story is no longer sad
since healing finally came
no one walks through recovery
and ever comes out the same.

What I Mean?

when I tell you, I LOVE YOU
I mean
I'll hold you, until
the moon kisses the night goodbye
and
I mean
I'll always
come back
like the
sun
breaking
through
the
sky.

You Filled Me.

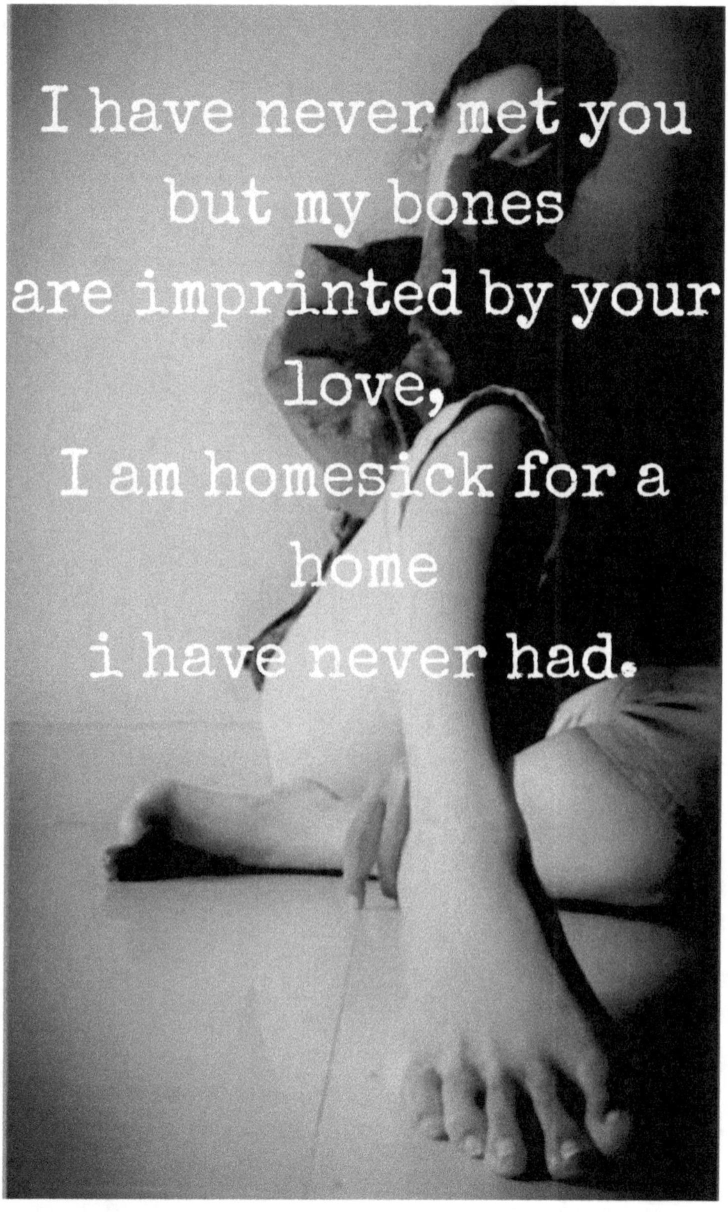

I have never met you
but my bones
are imprinted by your
love,
I am homesick for a
home
i have never had.

History Of Man Made Things

'Just man-made things'

This and that
What and how
And words myriad .
Confined to the cages
Of man-made meanings
In the past , present and coming ages.
Optimistic of breaking through
one day ,From soggy brains
With a pointy nose of a shrew
To paint a unfamiliar canvas
Where

Day could mean night
Love could mean hate
Life could mean death
Where
There's no you or me
There's no true or false
There's no white or black
There's no forever

All there is
Is a endless hollow, full of
words
Sailing through the dense
pillow of air
Contemplating, if humans
could care
Any lesser,

On affixing a meaning to
Words and things
And anything
And everything.

Cloud.

A cloud of sadness,
That covers my happiness.
It does not let me see the sun's
rays,
It does not let me breathe
An unexpected brightness
dazzles,
A big smile and warm hands,
They give me back that lost
happiness,
They were the same as I felt,
The first time I started crying.

Hope.

AS LONG AS
LOVE REMAINS RAME
AND DREAMS ARE FREE
I SHALL FALL FOR HOPE
A THOUSAND TIMES
THE SAME

HOPE

The Shadows Of Tulips

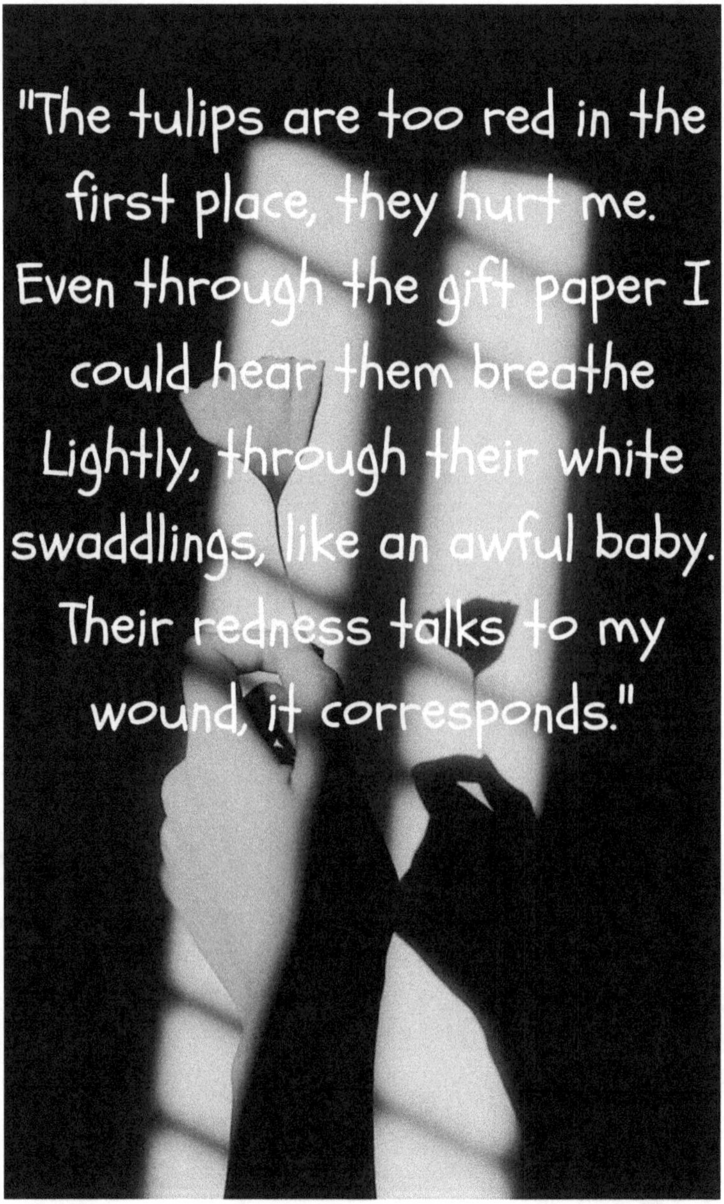

"The tulips are too red in the
first place, they hurt me.
Even through the gift paper I
could hear them breathe
Lightly, through their white
swaddlings, like an awful baby.
Their redness talks to my
wound, it corresponds."

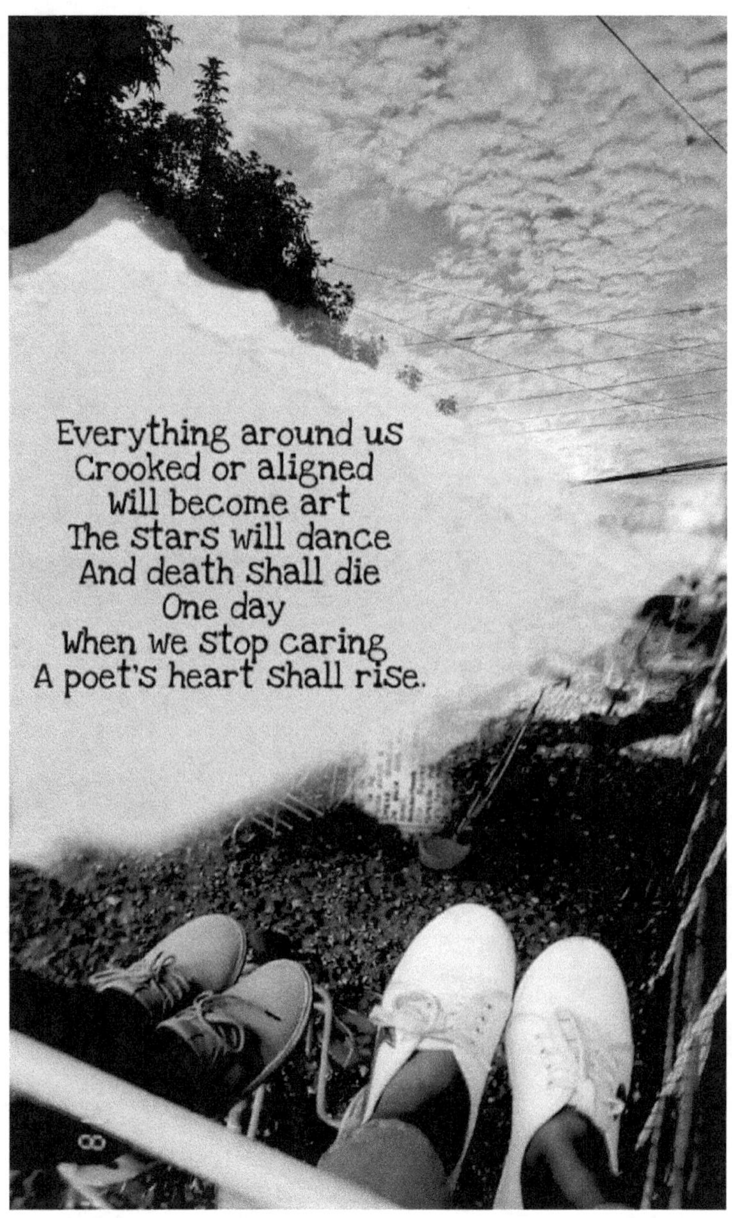

Everything around us
Crooked or aligned
Will become art
The stars will dance
And death shall die
One day
When we stop caring
A poet's heart shall rise.

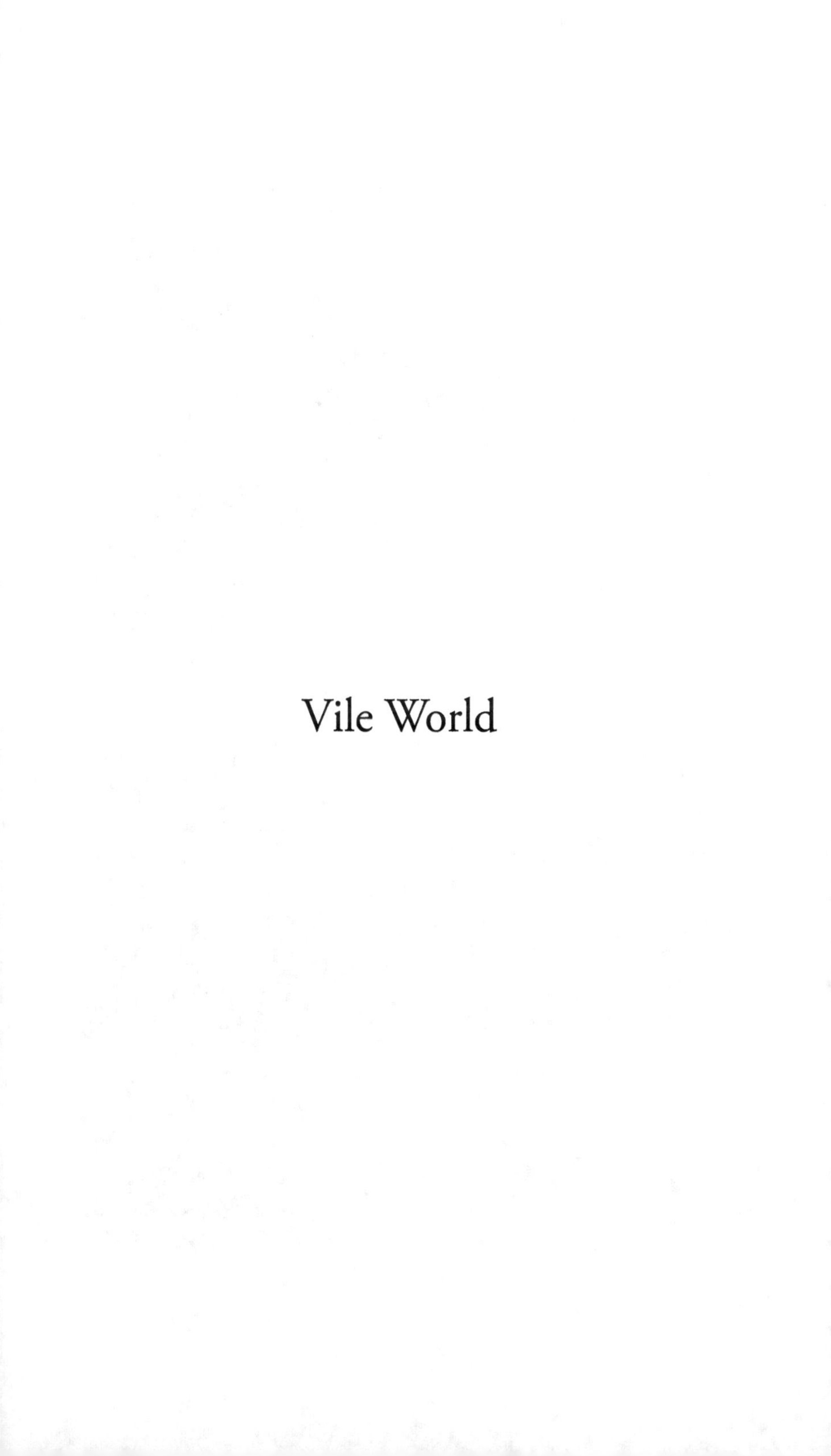

Vile World

"No longer mourn for
me when I am dead
Then you shall hear the
surly sullen bell
Give warning to the
world that I am fled
From this vile world,
with vilest worms to
dwell:"

Crushed Leaves.

No matter the land I walk
eyes only rummage love
Between wall cracks and
crushed leaves
Wandering souls and
any breeze
'Tis everywhere, yet not

Perhaps, if I wanted less
I'd have it all.

What I Feel.

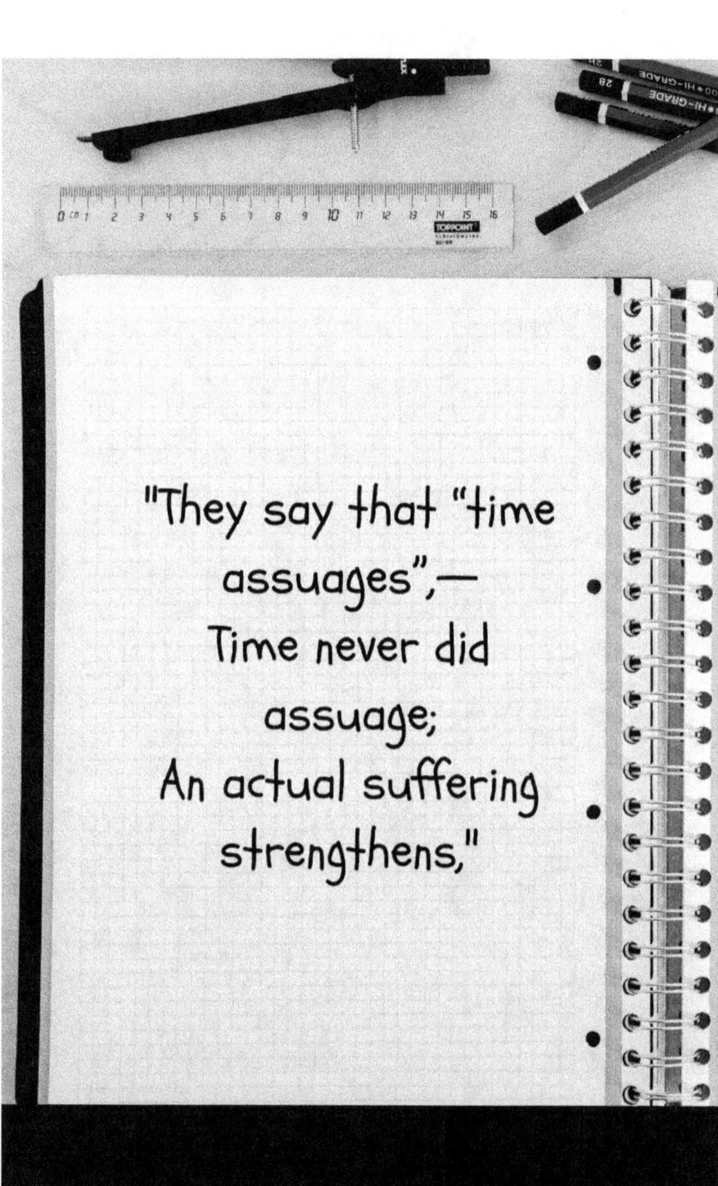

"They say that "time assuages",—
Time never did assuage;
An actual suffering strengthens,"

True?

it's true

1Ove always triumphs over

hate

yet

it's all fire and flames

when

everything of you it

overpowers and overtakes

Christmas trees

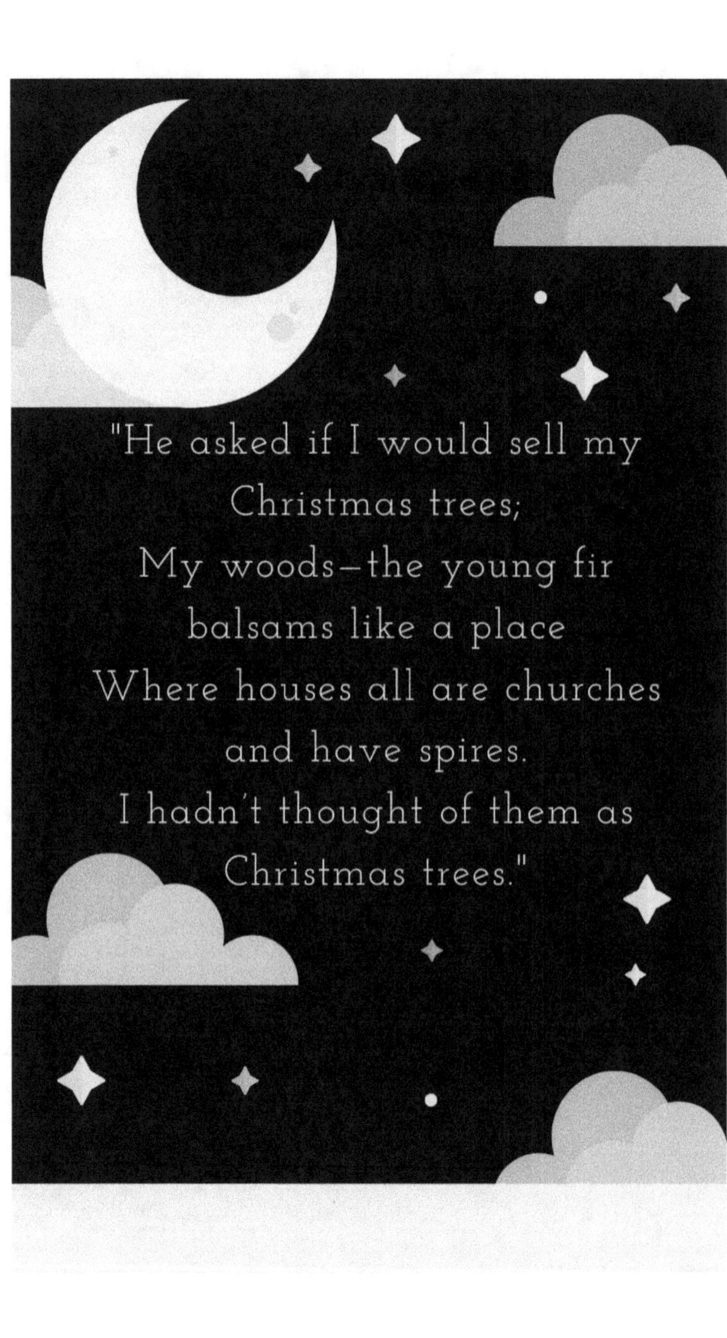

"He asked if I would sell my
Christmas trees;
My woods—the young fir
balsams like a place
Where houses all are churches
and have spires.
I hadn't thought of them as
Christmas trees."

Her

I'm scared to be scared
For, everything I ever wanted
Will one day, stand right in my face
And I'll inexorably be lost in my soul
For, my lips shall become
burial grounds of
Unsaid words and unsung
allegories
For, my heart would be
too consumed of fear
to ever risk love
For, my dreams shall
never see reality
For, one day I
shall die
trapped inside a jar
with a burning soul
Like a forgotten
firefly

Why Not I with thine?

"Nothing in the world is single;
All things by a law divine
In one spirit meet and mingle.
Why not I with thine?-"

Broken peices

There are different kinds of broken
Like peices of shattered glass
Some sharp and hard to mend
some crumpled with no comprehend

Waves

"A drop fell on
the Earth
Another on the
roof;
A half a dozen
kissed the
eaves,
And made the
gables laugh."

Life.

EVENING EDITION - JUN 14th 1942

DAILY NEWS

Time, in this
world, can only be
so much as can be
life
Darkness only so
much as can be
light

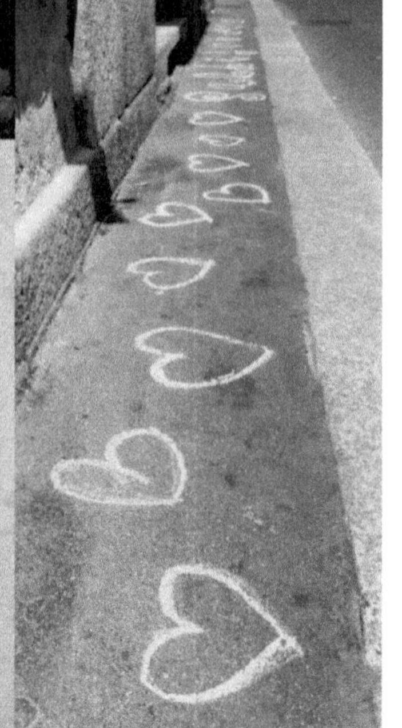

Hate, in this world, can only
be so much as can be loved
Humanity, only so much as can
be blood.

hope, in this world, can last
only so much as can endeavor
Agony, only so much as forever

Death, in this world, can
only be so much as birth
Art, only so much as earth

Nights.

My night is not as peaceful as your's,
you sleep with smile
i sleep with tears,
you have sweet dreams
I have trauma,
You wake up with beauty
I wake up thinking what to face today,
It's nice that we both live in the same world
but under the same world why god gave me
this life
and to you a happy one..
am i not his child?
am i not his angel?
all alone facing these dark has made me to kill
myself
so that i don't think of you nor this world.

Don't Look Out.

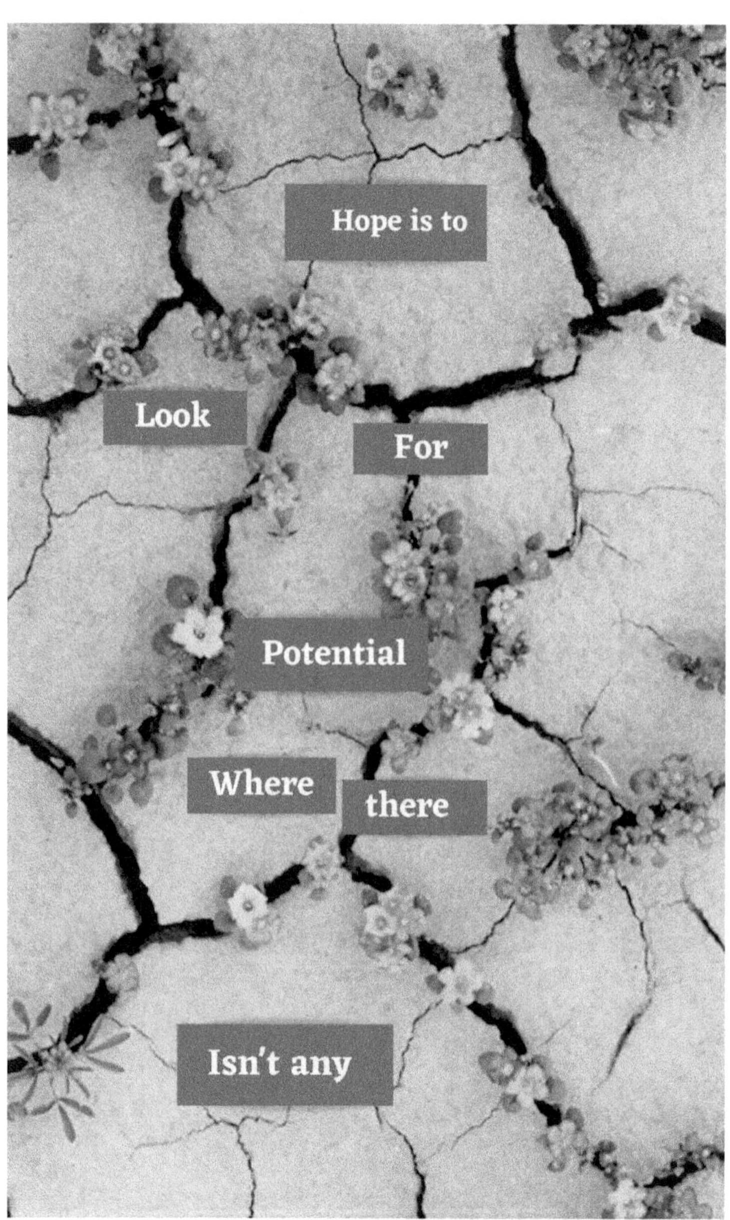

Hope is to
Look
For
Potential
Where
there
Isn't any

Fresh Way

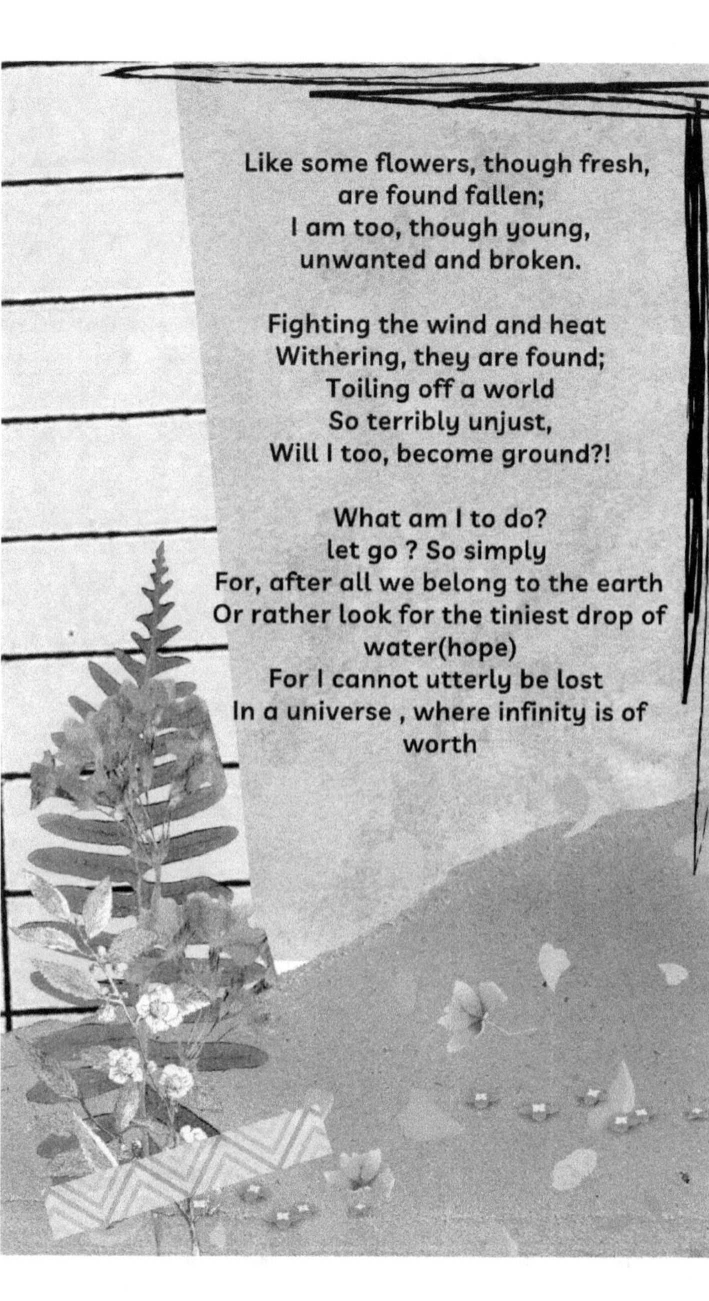

Like some flowers, though fresh,
are found fallen;
I am too, though young,
unwanted and broken.

Fighting the wind and heat
Withering, they are found;
Toiling off a world
So terribly unjust,
Will I too, become ground?!

What am I to do?
let go ? So simply
For, after all we belong to the earth
Or rather look for the tiniest drop of
water(hope)
For I cannot utterly be lost
In a universe , where infinity is of
worth

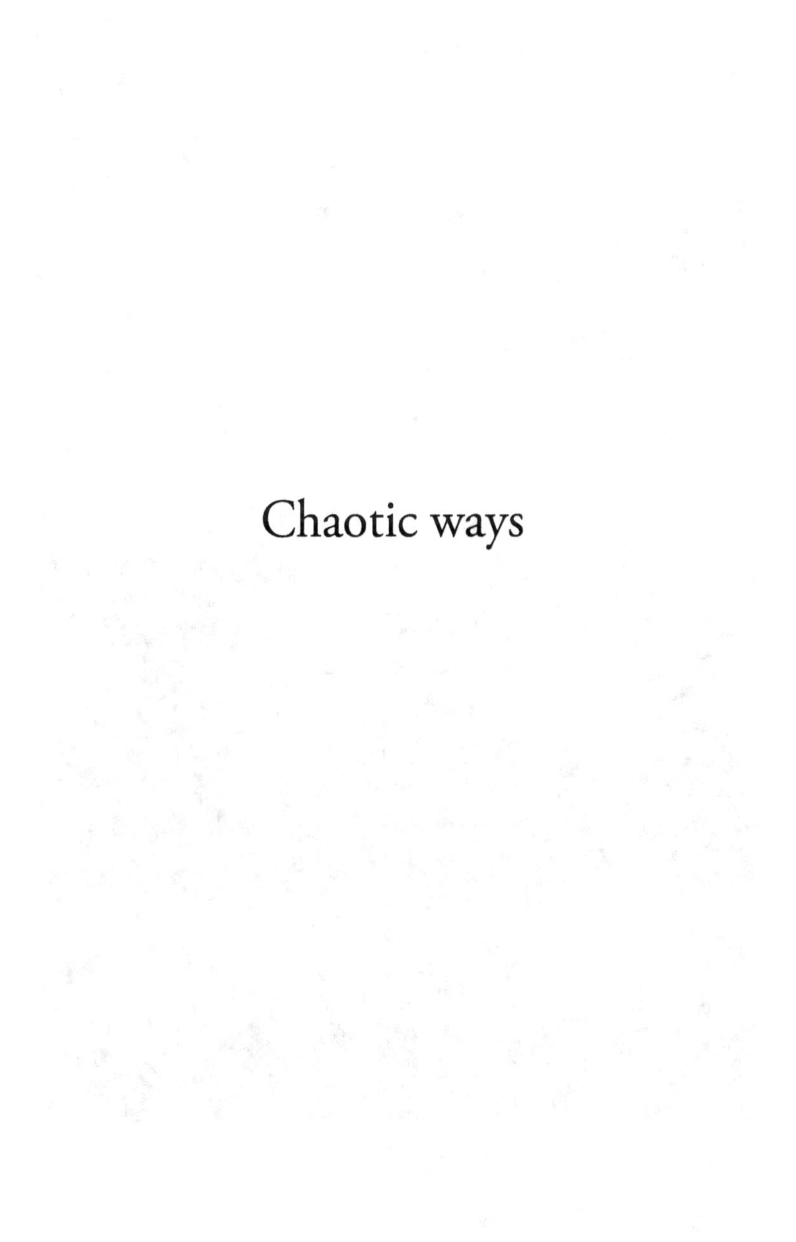

Chaotic ways

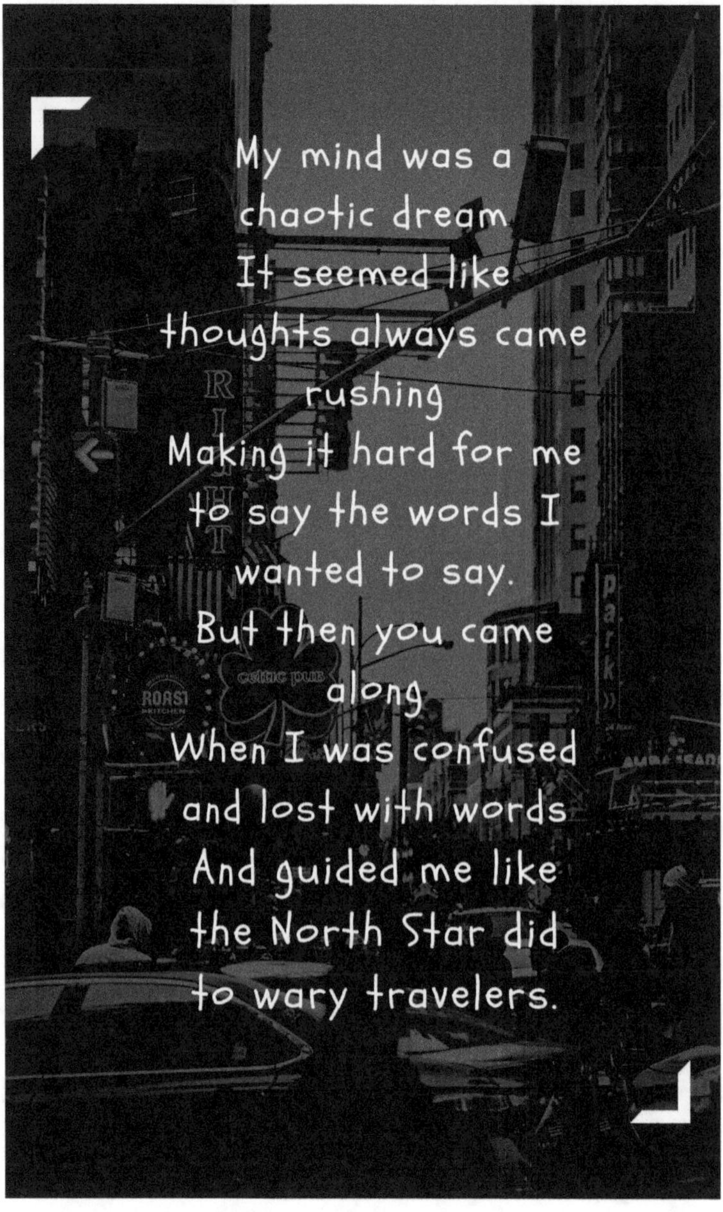

My mind was a
chaotic dream
It seemed like
thoughts always came
rushing
Making it hard for me
to say the words I
wanted to say.
But then you came
along
When I was confused
and lost with words
And guided me like
the North Star did
to wary travelers.

Near or Far?

You're so many miles away
So many, so many
I yearn a hug
A hand to hold
One glance of love
So much untold
You're so many miles away
So many, so many
Lie only words, between us
Yet our minds collide
For centuries we've known, as if
This one heart and it's tides

Evil

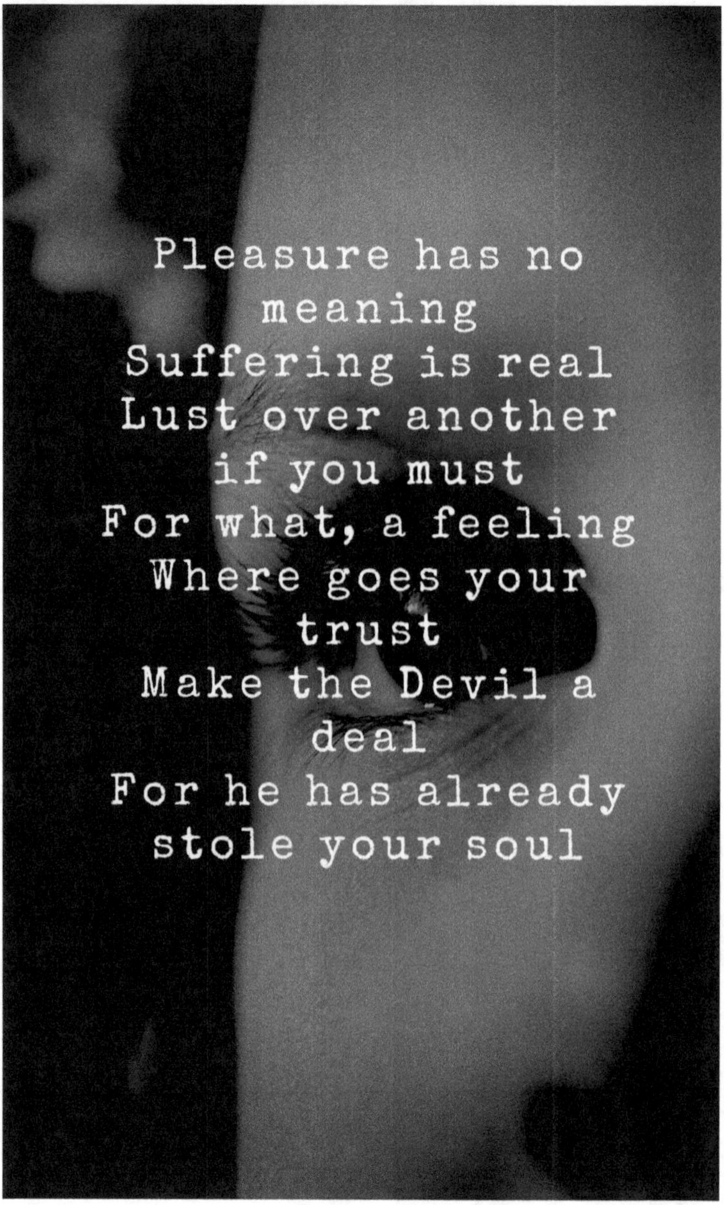

Pleasure has no
meaning
Suffering is real
Lust over another
if you must
For what, a feeling
Where goes your
trust
Make the Devil a
deal
For he has already
stole your soul

Habits

SOME HABITS
ARE HARD TO BREAK;
WALLS DIFFICULT TO PENETRATE.
YOU ARE TRAVELING UPHILL,
UNTIL YOU AREN'T
AND JUST LIKE THAT, SOME MEMORIES
ARE ENGRAVED IN THE SUBCONSCIOUS
WHERE MUSIC STILL PLAYS
THAT OLD SONG
THAT OPENS WOUNDS,
SPARKS VOICES

SAYING YOU ARE NEVER ENOUGH.

HUSH THE WINDS,
PICK UP THE PIECES
FROM ALL THE PLACES YOU FELL
AND LAY THEM DOWN.
THE WEIGHT IS NOT YOURS
TO CARRY.

I Write for You.

I always meant to write to you
But every time I'd start
The words came from some other place
Instead of from my heart

I know we had our share of fights
Especially in the end
That doesn't change the good times lost
Or the fact you were my friend

So here is my apology
As best as I know how
I've missed you then
I've missed you since
And I even miss you now

From: MARY MAGDALINA

I look into the mirror

To see myself and I

gaze up and down my face

at the wrinkles and the lines

I think of what I was

and what I grew to be

all my flaws and positives

I hope that others see

I look into a mirror

to study my own heart

to me I am myself

to others I am Mary